A Sunday Afternoon Drive

A Sunday Afternoon Drive

Wesley Jones

Wesley Jones
wesbjones08@gmail.com

ISBN 9781709928659

Printed in the United States of America

First Printing, 2020

Cover Art Designed by Megan Fowler
Author Photo by Audrey Odonkor

Editing: Tell Tell Poetry | www.telltellpoetry.com
Design: Cover&Layout | www.coverandlayout.com

To my family who encourages my absurdities, and to my friends who tolerate my manifestos, thank you for using an unhinged door

A Sunday Afternoon Drive

Contents

The Mark

I found a lone fly
Trapped as a lie
In a book I've only read.

Thought fails to recall,
Resting thin walls,
Upon the pilot's head.

Perhaps wings beat
Within folds of white sheets
Of the book before my bed.

So lies a smudge,
Few eyes would judge,
Still . . . I wish it were lead.

Wandering and Wondering

An empty road makes the sky
All the more worth looking at,
Especially when the wind is shy,
Especially when the road is flat.

At attention stands firm corn.
Meadow flowers front the bees.
A single cloud drifting forlorn
Intimidates the postured trees.

This road, endless, straight to heaven
Sure enough must reach this cloud—
Fleecy glacier, tranquil essence,
Born to drift and enshroud
Alone in the overarching ocean.
I wonder what must be found
that causes sole devotion?

For the help of more would surely aid
A scavenger hunt through terraced land,
But gaining a group always delays
The departure of important plans.

Thus it floats, my ivory ghost.
Yearning soft the world to drone.
When searching for what means the most,
A cloud is wise to go alone.

Timing

You can fight the world in a day
You can feel it burn in an hour
You can freeze to death in a minute
But you can fall in love in a second

A City Boy's Natural Wonder

My Aurora Borealis is the small dull Sun
Who shares warmth with cold streets.

My Everest is met with latter feet;
From its peak I watch the city buzz.

My Grand Canyon is packed with tons
Of treasures that stink in the heat.

My Great Barrier Reef
Sits by my bed. It's a home to one.

My Paricutin Volcano smokes
Forever on top of the mill.

My Harbor at Rio holds fewer boats—
My favorite's named *Brazil*

My Victoria Falls floats
In the park, spitting free at will.

But my world is full of those
Who will never see these thrills.

To Sit and To Smile

"The simple things in life are best."
To that I swaying agree.
For something hides in shadows cast
By simplicity.
Consider sitting and smiling
And how a thought can call
A physical warmth
(How logic free)
All from a joyful, curling chin
And an ivory painted jaw.
So I sit
I picture fair faces of friends
Smiles of smiles recalled.
"The simple things in life are best."
Simply—they aren't so simple at all.

Psalm 3:06

I tried to disbelieve
Yet found no evidence.
Like any good scientist
I sought to prove my theory
With infallible figures,
But in testing I discovered
My hypotheses were null
And my disobedient experiments
Confirmed the conclusion
I sought to disprove.

Come, let's go through it step by step:

First, I signed a contract to society
And lurked in the presence
Of the natural laws.
Yet soon I supposed,
"If here's the law,
Then who's the judge?"
I quickly left philosophy for physics.

I spanned to the Big Bang
And offered my heart to energy—
Pure, warm thermodynamics
Which can never leave me
(Nor anything for that matter.)
And speaking of matter—
Indestructible,
Irreproducible,
Indispensable,
Irr . . .
This house built upon sand
I deserted in the cosmos.

I escaped inward for shelter.
I took to my marrow and veins.
Journeying deeper and deeper.
Stumbling upon my code,
I fell in love with my intricacy—
"How complex and wonderfully made . . . "
The joy morphed to insecurity
At the site of a programmer's hand.
I took to a jog this time.

I caught my breath in the shadow
Of a wooden wishbone.
The leaves were lemons
(An apt venue for a sour man)
And as they dropped in abundance
The tree looked to be jumping in itself
And the leaves' ends curled to form
Slender champagne glasses,
Toasting to Creation.
Now it was a full-on sprint!

Chugging into the heat I cried,
"Why does ill strike good?"
This train dismantled immediately,
For the inquiry alone implied
A superior conductor fervently
Setting the two tracks apart.

With my last bit of strength, I crawled
Once more to the foot of the Universe
And tried to adopt
Billions of years for good measure . . .
"But at this rate," I collapsed,
"I might as well concede omnisciency."

And then, for the first time:

I exhaled death and breathed in life
(Forgetting carbon and oxygen).
I updated my code of humility.
I tipped my hat to the noble judge.
I embraced the warm hands of eternity.
I whispered to beauty, "You are no accident."
I toasted to creation with the Golden Maple.

Lists, Reminders, and Disappointments

This is the poem that I'll never publish
On the document that I'll never show
To anyone, save my mother or lover.

On my phone, the reminders hold lists
That frighten me to open.
Many of the scrolls include
Ideas for activities I rather enjoy.

I used to write my goals
On a massive dry-erase board,
But stopped when I kept expunging them
At midnight with unwashed hands
And the sediment would parachute to land
On the stack of motivational books.
(Worn out covers with unturned pages.)

The difference between us and them—
Those who execute their destiny
Crossing off life like a trip to the grocery
Daily inching their golden game piece forward—
Is the same disparity
between the Sun and the Moon.

No matter what the day brings
They rise and push on till conclusion.
Soaring higher and higher,
Beating down in brilliance.
And then,
When tuckered out by accomplishment,
Resting out of our way, finally,
We emerge to glow to ourselves.

Watchtower

I'd like to be a lighted tower.
For a night, the earth I'd scour
And save a lost soul if so lucky.
I'd see him in the distance bucking.

Once at shore he'd climb my steps
To tell the story of those depths
Who tossed him how a Wiffle ball
Is thrown to neighbors in the Fall.

The pitcher, a lad with backwards hat
And a ratty jersey time had lapsed.
It was his dad's, long before he
Put down his glove and took to sea.

Property

I have a periodic tendency,
Or is it a periodic tenancy,
To hold my heart like an old estate
Far from trespass, behind drab gates.

Absent chance for tenant's rent,
This stoic structure stuck to me.
A never transferred rotting gift
Absent of all privity.

It is a selfish life estate,
Uneasy for an easement.
But how could I entrust my fate
To a bond of sure defeasance?

With concurrent ownership out of question,
I offer myself this rare possession
For if acquired fair or adversely,
The original owner would be at the mercy

Of an occupant with perpetuity
Whose apparent authority could confuse
And rights would eventually suffuse.
No—eviction's my only security.

But maybe one day I'll leave it mislaid,
While my interests are elsewhere springing.
A bona-fide purchaser, in good faith, could pay
And up my estate she'd be bringing

The deed for me the grantor to sign
(Oh how I missed the ripe accession),
Though this title unexpected
Forever entrusted to her possession

So without limitation,
Abandonment with such sensation
Would possess and set me fee
And rid me of my property.

Wooden Contradiction

for Mooda

What of a rocking chair resolves one's soul
When bodies sway on wooden seas?
How does a bobbing chair lead the mind home?
Why feelings pensive, charming, serene?

Where else can one nostalgically cradle
Which revives ancient half-heard fables?
Who supposed rendering a thing unstable
Would in fact, deem it all the more able?

Leaf Alive

I went to step a leaf today
That was no leaf at all.
Instead, a charlatan painted green
(More vibrant than an Irish spring)
With shape of lizard more than toad
Escaped with ease as I heel-toed.
So bold the dance (a boxer's weave)
An audience of one in turn was pleased
With leaps and bounds at leaps and bounds
And all around with dart and shoot
The trickster did but all elude
Most every boot in town.
It was as if he forward knew
The landing lanes of dropping planes
Encroaching with a wistful sound
That if heard would never change
A confident decision made.
Fierce and unafraid
He pledged forth the foot of fate
A magic trick to turn the gait,
Yet in prestige the trickster found
An unknown fan of ample strength
Clapping quick to ground.
And when the final act commenced
The settling dust revealed a dense
Illusionist, bent and bowed.
There's something to be said
For a magician, a creature, a man,
Who would give everything
To a one-man crowd

The Tyrconnell Goldmine
(Far North Queensland, Australia)

A path whose only craft
Was the precedent of travelers last
Led to forsaken shafts
Well within the Outback.

Once for trench, now for tour,
Three abodes the dry land bore,
None of which held a door—
Such wind- and guest-swept corridors.

But being students without rent,
We pitched a plan to pitch a tent
And stole downhill with little sense
In search for phosphorescence.

Our camp was nothing, plus two stalls.
"Boys are soldiers, girls are dolls.
Fair dinkum. Natural Law."
Maxims of old Cher and Paul,

Our humble keepers at the time
Who spoke in austere Aussie lines,
Who cared as deeply as their mine,
And cooked all day for supper time.

After feasts the sky would set
Divinity's patient, casting net,
So testing Fisher once we bet
We'd catch first light mountain crests.

But alas, the Seaman won—
Golden mackerel to the sun
Whose gold and orange paint perfect run
Into that visual medicine.

Soon, a second dose would take
While looking up for Heaven's sake.
Who knew the Universe could bake
A powdered sugar blackened cake,

And just as such, so bittersweet,
Be the wonder that you greet
Reeling Glory's beaming fleet
Reeling Glory's beaming fleet.

And staring mute you have to hail the
King of captains, the One who sailed the
Sparks through space to sweet Australia—
Cosmic tears for fresh Vidalias.

The Present

I ponder of the Present
(Doubtful its presence at all).
Can a moment truly be captured
If the clock's hand never stalls?

Even if mid-through the word you reckon,
'Pre' has departed, 'sent' is to beckon
How scents of fir spread first-snow pastures
While a shadow-owl drifts to his master.

The Past forever recalled on.
Days devoured by locus.
Seconds inevitably elude us,
Despite unblinking focus.

Even if mid-through the word you reckon,
'Pre' has departed, 'sent' is to beckon
How scents of fir spread first-snow pastures
While a shadow-owl drifts to his master.

The Future awakens the fringes.
Morning horizon of the sea
Met with utter resistance
Emerging emphatically.

Even if mid-through the word you reckon,
'Pre' has departed, 'sent' is to beckon
How scents of fir spread first-snow pastures
While a shadow-owl drifts to his master.

So where is the precious Present?
Perhaps between summers it falls.
Can a moment truly be captured?
Did the clock's hand ever stall?

The Torture of Inaction (Turtle Xing)

With every step the traveler leaned,
And near the outskirts, refusing cane and cage
He dared to cross white into No Man's Land.
As the road condensed, the brown blur green'd,
I then made out the shelled old sage.

His wrinkles compounded (skin stretched by wisdom)
And dense in mud cake,
The excavated tortuous
Stomped his pegs in a forceful rhythm
That made the earth beneath him quake.

Our eyes met in time (for a thin hair of it),
And though brief, they spoke at length:
That he desired not a quest
But the hand of a Samaritan.
Nonetheless, he'd never ask nor thank

So 'twas a draw—eyes unlocked,
And we kept to our own in the dust.
Threw vapid June air,
Strangers flocked,
Golden rule to rust.

Soon I glanced in reflection
And still crept the antique box,
But oh, how another
Sped with aggression
Toward the mobile moss.

Who knows where he was lunging to
Or what from he was running,

But tires rolled cement up
Vengefully as they drew
Toward the mark they were shunning.

At their final rotation, my eyes fleeted
But my ears didn't—I hear the *crack* to this day
In every floor (more inside than outdoors)
And every perch of wooden seating
Echoes a crack, that road, and my way.

Now once more, I sigh to mourn
The consequence of prideful idle.
For I should have slain
Or been a savior that morn
Along that concrete isle.

Altered Idioms

A lie for a lie makes the whole world kind.
Break a leg, then see a doctor.
The pineapple doesn't fall far from the beach
A watched pot needs some foil.
A penny saved is a Denny's earned.
Grime flies when you have the runs.
Don't count you chickens before they rematch.
Don't put all your legs in one casket.
Always see the glass half-full—
Except when you're my waiter.
Great mimes think in sight.
Don't judge a crook by his lover.
The early bird may get the worm,
But the second mouse gets the cheese!

A Dove Poem

Even disheveled, she's a semblance of beauty.
Eyes are a portal, a glare all-consuming.
And despite displaying a calm disposition,
A passionate fire is covertly fuming.

Always astute and present to listen
A madam, a scholar, well-versed and well-written.
With a soothing voice, true to its style,
So is her soul—unique consistence.

Easy words pouring through smiles
'Round pillars crafted in arduous trials.
A woman of resilience will be my love—
Resilience, fused with the heart of a child.

On the worst days we will laugh just because!
On the grand days we will laugh just because!
(Not to mention, her Levi's fit like a glove)
Wise as a serpent, soft as a dove.

Ode to Frost

Faced with instability, instability, instability.
Did I give up or was it humility?
When will I be the "Bold" that fortune favors?
Yes, good fences make good neighbors
So I construct grand walls thickly layered
With calloused concrete.
I yearn razing my great Berlin . . . shame
My barriers unfazed by the hands of men.

But why not have a partner for the path overgrown?
Why not watch the woods fill up with snow
In unison, four eyes gazing in awe,
As opposed to a pair spectating alone?

Alas! An open heart's nay a weakness.
Never again content in the speechless
Now is the day for vulnerability—
For is that not the core of humanity?
Come, find the flesh of Achilles' heel,
None find love while carrying a shield.

Of Lust and Plunder

Without a world of covetous sex,
Think what could be accomplished?
Without the tempt of Passion's breast,
How straight would be thy compass?
Consider the reckless damage caused
Simply for sensation.
Pleasure's never worth its flaws;
I preach "no-creation."
No more wars with Helen of Troy,
Flesh addictions forsaken.
Gone you men who smile coy.
Purity safe from their taking.
Time once squandered, now so free,
What benefit to science.
The hours for you, cherished for me—
"Emersonian self-reliance."
Lust is the flaw of humanity, but in lieu
Of it, I shall conquer its habits.
But soon, I start desiring you—
A temple to be ravished.

A Wedding Escape (A Feat of Feet)

I.

The balls of my feet beat brutally
like the face of a crimson hammer
held by a lad at the fair
with white sleeves rolled to conviction
the young Sampson throws his wheat-fed frame
towards Hades' winning anaconda
attempts to slither the line but contracts
arms upward building fierce like a tower
of Babel to crash again against nerves

Ten passengers stride to keep calm
(conserving air they oppose expansion)
but the constricted toes bump
awfully aboard the throbbing subway
what's sowed is reaped inevitably
a traveler spills what feels like coffee
so brewed steam spreads and sticks
to the walls as a sludge-brown frog
pastes itself on Egyptian bricks

Missed is soaking in summer's heat
(not soaking in mist) but like summer nights
where boys disobey playing hide-and-seek
so Adam sweats behind the eve
panting dogs swell tighter causing commotion
prisoners in straitjackets try to strip jackets
ankles throw shackles at Cole Haan walls
covered in slimy streams of self-wetting
the guard cannot help though he wishes to
since black leather is required at a wedding
(funny how you'll buy a suit but not a shoe)

II.

The caned dance (as do the able) momentarily
a soft harp and soft rose able distract
till popping penguins corked campaign
and caesar wraps overarch with lament
to remind of an agonized pedal-corset
full in substance fuller in situation
a creamed cloth meets cream plate
a dreamed hand kisses dream date
a freed man oversteps free gates

Into the shadows of large leafless webs
or did a great army of witches on brooms
crash to the ground only to leave
sweeping faces facing the moon
and are minute mountains of thin piled greens
a cushioned path for Goliath's creep
which lead a body to wet dancing bodies
presented by stones too small to dent feet
(party favors wrapped later in sheets)

Laced serpents finally split asunder
thanks to the hurl of David's sling
shoes greet nature's phone-wire back
interwoven drooping ever so crooked chosen
by the crooked arm of a wooden-waiter
waiting to peal that damp tight skin
which itches later and itches then
now wadded indefinitely in perfect sphere
for what can escape infinity

But the cores which bondage failed
to clasp (inscribed as if a river map)
naturally then cool wade and smack
the luscious lips of fluid glass
beneath moist rings loose and pure

while free-flows would find others doom
souls find freedom in liquid ice
Hell for some's a paradise—
a way of life away of life

Boots in the Snow

I examined the broken walls of her russet boots
As they floated lightly atop the runoff rill
The little canoes weren't anything to remember,
But the trip that ensued
The moment my eyes picked up a paddle
And navigated cautiously up winding thighs,
Past a slant cotton opening
Where a sly belly button winked from,
Next amongst blooming hills
Finally arriving to a gentle delta
Perched ajar ever so enticingly—
(Daring for pursuit)—
Now that journey was remarkable.

But at first launch
The boat took a leak
And I forget the bucket
I was told to bring.
I sank faster than the densest metal,
Faster than a wounded eagle,
Faster than I ever admitted to anyone.

Right as I chomped hook, line, and sinker
The fisher(wo)man abandoned ship,
And just like a pair of red cowboy boots
Soaking in the storm
I too stood an exposed ruby soul

Love v. Not Love

Unable to still my violent ocean breast
Pith undulating, for a plum
Gently molds within my chest
She sighs a cool, delicious hum
v.
Jammed, these crooked pieces of puzzle.
The only thing sleeping tonight is my arm.
Choking on infinite hair—Rapunzel,
All you met was my wit and my charm.

The Breakup Paradox

It's unfair to be envious,
When you've moved on to the new,
But still I find myself jealous.

Maybe it's a primal trait
Of possession and pride.

Maybe it's because
A piece of a moment
Or two
Still lies near,
Just as you.

Rationality often wins,
And if I had it back
I would certainly reject it,
But still I find myself jealous.

Wanting to criticize,
The next to inherit you,
"I want you to be happy"—
Is that honestly true?
I want you to be happy,
But not happier than we—
That's the fairer of the two.

What guides my heart
In such odd ways,
I will never know,
Through and through

Although I sit here
Not wanting to,
Still I find myself jealous.

Defeat

Options arise when dining Defeat—
Overcome, or let letdown eat.
The table is set, portions undivided.
Will you or failure be first to the feast?

*

Antithesis

Clouds weep for the world
An ocean of tears
Yet the Sun is a tissue,
And gloom disappears.

Food never cherished,
Until you have starved.
Who would enjoy the night sky
If it were nothing but stars?

Love is nothing without hate,
So yes, God permits evil.
Without the dance of just and wrong
Automatons would be, not people.

And without its foil there is no beauty,
Life breathes antithesis
For without lies,
What would the truth be? Worthless.

A Funeral

She used to speak with such melodies
And a subtle bit of irony.
Peers would sneer at with jealously
For her faces were all worth desiring.

I weep for an old companion.
Someone I love is defunct.
She once held depths of a canyon,
Yet flooded, now lies sunk.

Drowned by pretentious diction.
Anchors: the words bought expensively.
Soul engulfed by fiction
She gasped, "Enlighted simplicity!"

I wish her assassins knew
That beauty's never full.
See Picasso's bull
Where beauty even bare
Transcends without a care—
How Wordsmith, Dorian, and Flake
Set you beautiful.

If your fathers lived, they would mourn,
"Darling no. How could they. Woe is me."
Perhaps like a phoenix born
But for now, rest in peace . . .

Gloom

There's a creature of sadness that summons a throe,
Burrowed deep a heinous crow.
Inward slashes, outward dull,
The creature of sadness that summons a throe.

There's a substance of sadness that poisons the brain,
Paintings and lyrics are mute to explain,
When tear-polished mirrors reflect only blame,
And the substance of sadness that poisons the brain.

There's a visage of sadness that weeps with dry eyes
Airing opaque, without surprise
Vacant of worth—more vacant of lies,
A visage of sadness that weeps with dry eyes.

If experienced, this sad seed you know
Certain seeds bud after been sown.
Dense black rose, nurtured by woe,
If experienced, this sadness you know.

Desolate

Me and the train are one and the same—
Alone in the moonlight, screeching insane.
Chugging eternally, we ache for rebuttal,
But no one reckons to cry back our name.

Dine

I kissed the sun goodnight then good morning.
After riding the pitch through country pitch-black,
I supposed it wise to sip something black—
Nice for low eyes a dim diner emerged.

I considered the slumped shack frail at first.
Burning out, the neon said: "Dine,"
So, I followed the cordial command
To a poor acting lot, who forgot all its lines.

The cracks led to an entrance. A body stood guard
Scissoring a cigarette, the password was "Mornin'"—
I would've humored the bum if I hadn't
Quit the night prior as I finished my pack.

Smoky windows revealed only a window
For a regular's convenience: "Nine—Noon"
They claimed to be servants of souls—
Or at least, servers of soul food.

As I parted the doors, something escaped.
Turned neck, but no blind dog chased the horizon,
My senses then whispered, "Though intangible it may be,
The creature you freed was the essence of bees."

I like to believe the bees kept in range
And dwelt homely in the hives of the heads
Of maternal waitresses, so as to explain
Sweet names like "Honey" smiled at strangers.

The red booths were likewise smile-torn to show
Plaqued padding of worn foam teeth.
Spoons held dry silhouettes of the past—
Contrary to belief, an indication of "Good."

And the table was cold to counter the food,
And the jukebox sighed an antique tune,
And the coffee was same to a smack on the face.
The sweet tea claimed everyone's teeth.

So I stayed, for a moment, more than allotted
In that crippled building which had forgotten
Some of itself—I too had forgotten,
"Wood and teeth often are better off rotten."

Riding Home from Grandma's

Laundry for sky
Light sheets swap dark
Smooth and mysterious
Gliding like sharks
Parental whispers
Young embers in back
The stalwart soft journeys
A safe that won't crack

Desserts become morphine
Wearing down patients
Engines and exhales
Homeostasis
Sporadic lights wink
Hypnosis ensues
Sandman soft-tempts
Reluctant, refused

Eyelids are shutters
Weighted by lead
Dozens of dozes
Coaxing limp heads
Slow photo snaps
Eye-lens to jam
Battle is over
Victor is sand.

"Yet the war was not won,"
Exclaim birds in the sun
Resurrecting the once fallen heads,
And full of drowsy amazement
Small bodies in stasis
Awake, once more, from the dead!

Of Humans and Foliage

Gazing with eyes intrusive,
Eve was dropping on town and trees,
Reaching a sharp conclusion
Of humanity, of leaves.

The masses file, content as if gates
Stemmed past the branches.
But unique in fields, shade, and shape,
Duets of wind toss dancers

Smile grandiose in the sun rays,
Traveling with nature's intent.
And with a smell so sweet on Sundays
Laughter rustles content!

Later, when the moon releases its glow
Tiptoeing to places unseen,
In night's breath, bodies throw
Against one another with ease.

But quickly, the breeze will freeze.

Sky-blue unrenewed
Epidermis dull and foggy,
Cold sweats of morning dew,
Curl a shivered body.

Falling unavoidably,
Returning whence grew,
Yet cascading ever so cordially
Vast riches pass down at tomb.

No longer coursing with veins
The once verdurous system,
Shrinking, cracking, in old age,
But oh, how we once glistened!

Upon Soaring (My First Plane Ride)

From a butterfly eye I witness the truth,
That things so grand are vastly minute.
A cloudy note floats to my root,
Muffle-toned, a tenor of flute

"Returning an ant, I greatly demise,"
I think peeking down with weary an eye.
"Nay the word 'speck' can justly describe
Creatures below scoped from the sky."
An epiphany elevates quick as I fly,

"In stratos, I, a remarkable centipede
Back on terrain—one in infinity
And with descent, my odds are diminishing
Of ever landing the archives of history."

"Vibrant and grand, let this poor beetle,"
I pleaded inward to the holiest steeple,
"Remain afloat where he can reign regal
Though endangered, even more lethal—
Returning a drop to an ocean of people."

Too Restless to Ever Dream

Enemy army advances,
Unbarbing final defenses.
Soldiers practice countless drills
(Men don't, but process forgets kills)
A value to the trenches.

Peasant-bee consumed in hive,
Frantic, buzzing, five-to-five,
For Queen wants double honey
Before tomorrow's sunny.
How minions cheerfully strive.

Conveyer-belt unceasing,
Piece piece piece-sing,
Forbidden slow or halt
Since wires should find fault,
And engines demand greasing.

Unblinking soldier, circling bee,
Perspiring machine—
Servants of distraction,
Reluctant to face a fraction,
Too restless to ever dream.

The Speckled Mare

I once knew a boy, who rode past a farm
And a mare on rolling green he viewed
Grazing innocence upon the yard.

Her silver coat of royal hue
Charmed the lovely hills
How scattered stars freckle through.

In growing time, the boy still
Considers that guileless mare
But now the memory issues chills.

He doesn't find fair, what first was fare
When gazing at species'd glory—
For avarice strips her winsome hair.

Or another glum story,
Stabled through night,
He wakes to her unstable roaring,

But perhaps the most horrific fright:
Instead of retired—glued and tired. A sad
shadow cast over shadowed might.

But maybe (just maybe) there still sits a lad
Somewhere of near, or perhaps far
Who kept at the farm with his glad

Who peers past pane in a dust-maroon car,
Who wanders gay with a speckled mare
Upon a naïve emerald yard.

An Evening Fountain

While foam-bursts erupt the occasion
We must raise a toast—
"Huzza to Spring!"
For stillness held a mirror of faces,
But luckily rings
Now shatter and boast.

While children leap through geyser recitals,
Lovers kiss on the side
(They hate it),
Grey men toss crumbs so vital
To pavement
For beaked pilots nearby.

While reverse waterfalls sparkle
Over the unheard quote
Sleeping at the base.
Cannons prove vocal
(In this case),
Sieging over the moat.

While eye-level with the kinetic peaks,
A philosopher spews tales
In Latin
(Perhaps Greek),
Lips chafed and robe crackin'
Solemn in center he hails.

While guarding glitters: diamonds and rubies
(Tricks deceive vision,
Thanks to wet acrobats),
And within the parade, "La Mer" by Debussy
Echoes in stride with the splash,
Postponing the waning orange—while it listens

About the Author

Wesley Jones, a jester to Kings, a Prince himself. Aware of his own existence. Disciplined, fluctuating, resilient—though drowning meekly as any other. Ungentle when holding a flower. A gentleman holding a door. Surging with red clay and red Coca-Cola. Son of a minister. Boy of a teacher. Youngest of three  and little brother to the world. Subtly managerial, a risk-adverse entrepreneur, practicing the law of Christ and man. Bulldog tenacious and elephant learned. Preferring electrons to neutrons—favoring protons to both. A poet by necessity to wrestle with God. Eager, one day, for a three-legged race.

Made in the USA
Columbia, SC
13 July 2020